# Hats & Ha
## for the family

MW00682839

Warm Hands, Warm Heart! Red Heart® Yarns have a long tradition of adding comfort, warmth, and style to our lives. Hats, scarves, mittens, and gloves are ideal projects to make throughout the year. They are not a huge commitment of time, and they make appreciated gifts for all ages. We are happy to share this collection of cozy designs to warm you and yours.

## About Red Heart Yarns

Red Heart is one of the most trusted brands in yarn. For over 75 years more people have chosen to make American heirlooms using Red Heart yarn than any other yarn. Red Heart yarns stand for quality, largest color selection, fashion and above all else, crafted with love. Whatever your creativity calls for, you'll find it in the Red Heart family.

LEISURE ARTS, INC.
Maumelle, Arkansas

# Strawberry Beret & Wrist Warmers

Designed by Kim Guzman.

 **EASY**

## SHOPPING LIST

**Yarn** (Medium Weight)
**RED HEART® With Love®**
- ☐ 1703 Candy Pink **A** - 1 skein
- ☐ 1907 Boysenberry **B** - 1 skein

## Crochet Hook
- ☐ 6.5 mm [US K-10½]

## Additional Supplies
- ☐ Yarn needle

# SIZE INFORMATION

**Finished Measurements**

**Beret:** 16{18}"/40.5{45.5} cm
in circumference
8½{10}"/21.5{25.5} cm in diameter
**Wrist Warmers:** 2¾{3¼}" wide x
3{3½}" long/7{8.25} cm x 7.5{9} cm

*Size Note:* Directions are written
in Blue for girl's size Small (2-4)
and in Green for size Large (6-8).
Directions written in Black apply
to both sizes.

# GAUGE INFORMATION

16 sts and 14 rows = 4" (10 cm)
**CHECK YOUR GAUGE. Use any
size hook to obtain the gauge.**

## ——SPECIAL STITCHES——

**shell:** (2 dc, ch 2, 2 dc) in same
space.
**sc2tog (single crochet
2 together):** [Insert hook in next
st, yo, draw yarn through st] twice,
yo, draw yarn through 3 loops
on hook.
**dc2tog (double crochet
2 together):** [Yo, insert hook in
next st, yo, draw yarn through
st, yo, draw through 2 loops on
hook] twice, yo, draw through
3 loops on hook.

**NOTE:** When working rows in back
loop only, if your last st is a little
loose, try working the last st into
both loops of st.

# BERET
## Band

With **A**, leaving an 8" (20.5 cm)
sewing length, ch 5{7}.

**Row 1:** Working in back bar of
each ch *(Fig. 3, page 44)*, slip st in
2nd ch from hook, slip st in each
ch across; turn – 4{6} slip sts.

**Row 2:** Working in back loops
only *(Fig. 4, page 44)*, slip st in
each st across; turn – 4{6} slip sts.

Repeat Row 2 until 106{114} rows
have been worked or band
measures 14{15}"/35.5{38} cm
from beginning. Do not fasten off.
Rotate to begin working along
sides of rows.
Work now progresses in rounds.

## Crown

**Round 1 (Right side):** Ch 1, work
64{80} sc evenly spaced across
side edge of band; join with a
slip st in first sc.

**Round 2:** Ch 3 (counts as dc here and throughout), skip first sc, dc in each sc around; join with a slip st in top of beginning ch-3 – 64{80} dc. Fasten off **A**.

**Round 3:** With right side facing, join **B** with a slip st in top of beginning ch-3; ch 1, sc in same st, *ch 2, skip next dc, sc in next dc; repeat from * around to last dc, ch 2, skip last dc; join with a slip st in first sc – 32{40} ch-2 spaces.

**Round 4:** Slip st in next ch-2 space, ch 1, sc in same ch-2 space, *shell in next ch-2 space**, sc in next ch-2 space; repeat from * around, ending last repeat at **; join with a slip st in first sc – 16{20} shells. Fasten off **B**.

**Round 5:** With right side facing, join **A** with a slip st in ch-2 space of any shell; ch 1, sc in same space as joining, ch 5, (sc, ch 5) in each ch-2 space around; join with a slip st in first sc – 16{20} ch-5 spaces.

**Round 6:** Slip st in next ch-5 space, ch 1, 5 sc in each ch-5 space around; join with a slip st in first sc – 80{100} sc.

**Round 7:** Ch 3, skip first sc, dc in each sc around; join with a slip st in top of beginning ch-3 – 80{100} dc.

### Size Large ONLY
**Round 8:** Ch 3, skip first dc, dc in each of next 2 dc, dc2tog over next 2 sts, *dc in each of next 3 dc, dc2tog over next 2 sts; repeat from * around; join with a slip st in top of beginning ch-3 – 80 dc.

### Both Sizes
**Round 8{9}:** Ch 1, sc in first st, sc in next 7 sts, sc2tog over next 2 sts, *sc in next 8 sts, sc2tog over next 2 sts; repeat from * around; join with a slip st in first sc – 72 sts.

**Round 9{10}:** Ch 1, sc in first st, sc in next 6 sts, sc2tog over next 2 sts, *sc in next 7 sts, sc2tog over next 2 sts; repeat from * around; join with a slip st in first sc – 64 sts.

**Round 10{11}:** Ch 1, sc in first st, sc in next 5 sts, sc2tog over next 2 sts, *sc in next 6 sts, sc2tog over next 2 sts; repeat from * around; join with a slip st in first sc – 56 sts.

**Round 11{12}:** Ch 1, sc in first st, sc in next 4 sts, sc2tog over next 2 sts, *sc in next 5 sts, sc2tog over next 2 sts; repeat from * around; join with a slip st in first sc – 48 sts.

**Round 12{13}:** Ch 1, sc in first st, sc in next 3 sts, sc2tog over next 2 sts, *sc in next 4 sts, sc2tog over next 2 sts; repeat from * around; join with a slip st in first sc – 40 sts.

**Round 13{14}:** Ch 1, sc in first st, sc in next 2 sts, sc2tog over next 2 sts, *sc in next 3 sts, sc2tog over next 2 sts; repeat from * around; join with a slip st in first sc – 32 sts.

**Round 14{15}:** Ch 1, sc in first st, sc in next st, sc2tog over next 2 sts, *sc in next 2 sts, sc2tog over next 2 sts; repeat from * around; join with a slip st in first sc – 24 sts.

**Round 15{16}:** Ch 1, sc in first sc, sc2tog over next 2 sts, *sc in next sc, sc2tog over next 2 sts; repeat from * around; join with a slip st in first sc – 18 sts.

**Round 16{17}:** Ch 1, *sc2tog over next 2 sts; repeat from * around; join with a slip st in first sc – 9 sts.

**Round 17{18}:** Ch 1, sc in first sc, *sc2tog over next 2 sts; repeat from * around; join with a slip st in first sc – 5 sts. Fasten off leaving a sewing length.

With yarn needle, weave sewing length through tops of sts in last round, gather top and secure.

## Finishing
With yarn needle and sewing length, sew brim seam. Weave in ends.

# WRIST WARMERS
(Make 2)
## Wrist Band
With **A**, leaving an 8" (20.5 cm) sewing length, ch 7{9}.

**Row 1:** Working in back bar of each ch *(Fig. 3, page 44)*, slip st in 2nd ch from hook, slip st in each ch across; turn – 6{8} slip sts.

**Row 2:** Working in back loops only *(Fig. 4, page 44)*, slip st in each st across; turn – 6{8} slip sts.

Repeat Row 2 until 38{42} rows have been worked or band measures 5{5½}"/12.5{14} cm from beginning. Do not fasten off. Rotate to begin working along side edge of wrist band. Work now progresses in rounds.

**Round 1 (Right side):** Ch 1, work 16{20} sc evenly spaced across side edge of band; join with a slip st in back loop only of first sc.

**Round 2:** Ch 3 (counts as dc here and throughout), working in back loops only, skip first sc, dc in each sc around; join with a slip st in top of beginning ch-3 – 16{20} dc.

**Round 3:** Ch 1, sc in first st, *ch 2, skip next dc, sc in next dc; repeat from * around to last dc, ch 2, skip last dc; join with a slip st in first sc – 8{10} ch-2 spaces.

**Round 4:** Slip st in next ch-2 space, ch 1, sc in first ch-2 space, *shell in next ch-2 space**, sc in next ch-2 space; repeat from * around ending last repeat at **; join with a slip st in first sc – 4{5} shells. Fasten off **A**.

**Round 5:** With right side facing, join **B** to remaining front loop of any sc in Round 1 *(Fig. 6a, page 45)*; ch 1, sc in same st as joining, *ch 2, skip next sc, sc in next sc; repeat from * around to last sc, ch 2, skip last sc; join with a slip st in first sc – 8{10} ch-2 spaces.

**Round 6:** Repeat Round 4. Fasten off **B**.

## Finishing
With yarn needle and sewing length, sew wrist band seam. Weave in ends.

# Boy's Hat & Scarf Set

Designed by Tracie Barrett.

 **EASY**

## SHOPPING LIST

### Yarn (Medium Weight)

**RED HEART® With Love®**

☐ 1401 Pewter **A** - 1 skein
☐ 1601 Lettuce **B** - 1 skein

### Crochet Hook

☐ 5.5 mm [US I-9] **and**
☐ 6 mm [US J-10]

### Additional Supplies

☐ Yarn needle

# SIZE INFORMATION

## Finished Measurements

**Hat:** 18{20}"/45.5{51} cm circumference by 8" (20.5 cm) long (without pompom)

**Scarf:** 5{6½}"/12.5{16.5} cm wide x 41½{51}"/105.5{129.5} cm long (without fringe)

*Size Note:* Directions are written in Blue for boy's size Small and in Pink for size Medium. Directions written in Black apply to both sizes.

# GAUGE INFORMATION

13 sts and 11 rounds = 4" (10 cm) with smaller hook;
12 sts and 10 rows = 4" (10 cm) with larger hook.
**CHECK YOUR GAUGE. Use any size hook to obtain the gauge.**

**NOTE:** Carry color not in use up inside of hat and up side of scarf after changing colors.

**NOTE:** Ch 2 does NOT count as a st.

# HAT

## Color Sequence

Following instructions below, work in the following color sequence:
[2 rounds **A**, 2 rounds **B**] twice,
3{4} rounds **A**, 4 rounds **B**,
5{4} rounds **A**, 2 rounds **B**,
[1 round **A**, 1 round **B**] twice,
1 round **A**.

With smaller hook and **A**, ch 2.

**Round 1 (Right side):** 8 Hdc in 2nd ch from hook; join with a slip st to first hdc.

**Round 2:** Ch 2, 2 hdc in each hdc around; join with a slip st in first hdc *(Fig. 5a, page 44)* – 16 hdc.

**Round 3:** Ch 2, [hdc in first hdc, 2 hdc in next hdc] 8 times; join – 24 hdc.

**Round 4:** Ch 2, hdc in each hdc around; join.

**Round 5:** Ch 2, [hdc in next 2 hdc, 2 hdc in next hdc] 8 times; join – 32 hdc.

**Round 6:** Ch 2, hdc in each hdc around; join.

**Round 7:** Ch 2, [hdc in next 3 hdc, 2 hdc in next hdc] 8 times; join – 40 hdc.

**Round 8:** Ch 2, [hdc in next 4 hdc, 2 hdc in next hdc] 8 times; join – 48 hdc.

**Round 9:** Ch 2, hdc in each hdc around; join.

**Round 10:** Ch 2, [hdc in next 5 hdc, 2 hdc in next hdc] 8 times; join – 56 hdc.

**Size Medium ONLY**
**Round 11:** Ch 2, [hdc in next 6 hdc, 2 hdc in next hdc] 8 times; join – 64 hdc.

**Both Sizes**
**Round 11{12}:** Ch 2, hdc in each hdc around; join.

**Rounds 12-20{13-20}:** Ch 2, hdc in each hdc around; join.

**Round 21:** Ch 2, hdc in front loop of each hdc around *(Fig. 4, page 44)*; join.

**Rounds 22-26:** Ch 2, hdc in each hdc around; join.
TURN at end of Round 26.

**Round 27:** Ch 1, sc in each hdc around; join. Fasten off.

## Finishing
Weave in ends. Using both **A** and **B**, make a 4" (10 cm) pompom *(Figs. 8a-c, page 46)*; attach to hat. Fold brim up at Round 21.

# SCARF

## Color Sequence
Following instructions below, work in the following color sequence: [2 rows **A**, 2 rows **B**] twice, *[4 rows **A**, 4 rows **B**] twice, [2 rows **A**, 2 rows **B**] twice; repeat from * 3{4} more times.

With larger hook and **A**, ch 16{20}.

**Row 1 (Right side):** Hdc in 2nd ch from hook and each ch across; turn – 15{19} hdc.

**Row 2:** Ch 2, hdc in each hdc across *(Fig. 5b, page 45)*; turn.

**Row 3:** Ch 2, hdc in each hdc across; turn.

**Rows 4-104{128}:** Repeat Row 3. Do not fasten off at end of last row, but turn to work edging.

## Edging
Ch 1, sc evenly around scarf, working 3 sc in corners; join with a slip st in first sc. Fasten off.

## Finishing

### Fringe

Cut 30{38}, 6" (15 cm) pieces each of **A** and **B**. Using one strand of each color in each stitch across both short ends, attach fringe along short edges of scarf: fold yarn in half forming a loop; insert the crochet hook through the fabric from the wrong side and draw the loop through, then draw the yarn ends through the loop and tighten *(Figs. 1a & b)*.

**Fig. 1a**

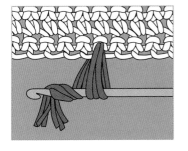

**Fig. 1b**

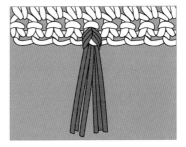

# Streetwise Brim Hat

Designed by Sharon Mann.

 **EASY**

**Finished Circumference
(at bottom edge):** 19½" (49.5 cm)

## SHOPPING LIST

**Yarn** (Medium Weight) **MEDIUM 4**

RED HEART® Soft®

☐  9440 Light Grey Heather - 1 ball

## Crochet Hook

☐  5 mm [US H-8]

## Additional Supplies

☐  Heavy-weight interfacing
or plastic for brim

☐  Stitch marker

☐  Yarn needle

## GAUGE INFORMATION

16 sc and 15 rounds = 4" (10 cm).
**CHECK YOUR GAUGE. Use any
size hook to obtain the gauge.**

**NOTE:** Hat is worked in
continuous rounds. Place marker
for beginning of round.

# HAT
## Crown

Ch 4; slip st in first ch to form ring.
Place marker for beginning of
round.

**Round 1 (Right side):** Work 6 sc in
ring – 6 sts.

**Round 2:** Work 2 sc in each st
around – 12 sts.

**Round 3:** [2 Sc in next st, sc in
next st] around – 18 sts.

**Round 4:** [2 Sc in next st, sc in
next 2 sts] around – 24 sts.

**Round 5:** [2 Sc in next st, sc in
next 3 sts] around – 30 sts.

**Round 6:** [2 Sc in next st, sc in
next 4 sts] around – 36 sts.

**Round 7:** [2 Sc in next st, sc in
next 5 sts] around – 42 sts.

**Round 8:** [2 Sc in next st, sc in
next 6 sts] around – 48 sts.

**Round 9:** Ch 3 (counts as dc here
and throughout), dc in same
space, dc in next 7 sts, [2 dc in
next st, dc in next 7 sts] around –
54 sts.

**Round 10:** [2 Sc in next st, sc in next 8 sts] around – 60 sts.

**Round 11:** [2 Sc in next st, sc in next 9 sts] around – 66 sts.

**Round 12:** [2 Sc in next st, sc in next 10 sts] around – 72 sts.

**Round 13:** [2 Sc in next st, sc in next 11 sts] around – 78 sts.

**Round 14:** Ch 3, dc in each st around.

**Rounds 15-18:** Sc in each st around.

**Rounds 19-28:** Repeat Rounds 14-18.

**Round 29:** Hdc in each st around; slip st in first st.
Fasten off.

# Brim
## TOP SIDE
Mark 22 sts on front of Hat on Round 29 for Brim.

**Row 1:** With right side facing, join yarn in first marked st; working in front loops only *(Fig. 4, page 44)*, sc in each of next 22 sts; turn.

**Row 2:** Ch 1, sc in each st across, sc in back loops in next 4 sts on Hat; turn – 26 sts.

**Row 3:** Ch 1, sc in each st across, sc in front loops in next 4 sts on Hat; turn – 30 sts.

**Row 4:** Ch 1, sc in each st across, sc in back loop in next st on Hat; turn – 31 sts.

**Row 5:** Ch 1, sc in each st across, sc in front loop in next st on Hat; turn – 32 sts.

**Row 6:** Ch 1, sc in each st across, sc in back loop in next st on Hat; turn – 33 sts.

**Row 7:** Ch 1, sc in each st across, sc in front loop in next st on Hat – 34 sts.
Fasten off.

**BOTTOM SIDE**
**Row 1:** With wrong side facing, join yarn on wrong side of Row 1 of Brim; sc in remaining back loops of first 22 sts *(Fig. 6a, page 45)*; turn.

**Row 2:** Ch 1, sc in each st across, sc in front loops in next 4 sts on Hat; turn – 26 sts.

**Row 3:** Ch 1, sc in each st across, sc in back loops in next 4 sts on Hat; turn – 30 sts.

**Row 4:** Ch 1, sc in each st across, sc in front loop in next st on Hat; turn – 31 sts.

**Row 5:** Ch 1, sc in each st across, sc in back loop in next st on Hat; turn – 32 sts.

**Row 6:** Ch 1, sc in each st across, sc in front loop in next st on Hat; turn – 33 sts.

**Row 7:** Ch 1, sc in each st across, sc in back loop in next st on Hat – 34 sts.
Fasten off.

**FINISHING**
Using Brim as a template, cut a piece of stiff interfacing or plastic to same dimensions. Slip piece in between layers of Brim and sew Brim closed.
Weave in ends.

# Charleston Cloche

*(Shown on page 21)*

Designed by Kim Guzman.

 **INTERMEDIATE**

### Finished Measurements

Hat: 21" (53.5 cm) circumference x 11" (28 cm) tall (unfolded)
Flower: 4" (10 cm) across (at widest)

## SHOPPING LIST

**Yarn** (Medium Weight)

**RED HEART® Soft®**

☐ 3720 Lavender - 1 ball

## Crochet Hook

☐ 5.5 mm [US I-9]

## Additional Supplies

☐ Yarn needle

# GAUGE INFORMATION

Round 1 of Hat = 1½" (4 cm) across; Rounds 1 and 2 of Hat = 2½" (6.5 cm) across.

**CHECK YOUR GAUGE. Use any size hook to obtain the gauge.**

## ——SPECIAL STITCHES——

**Beg-Cl (beginning cluster):** (first leg) Yo, insert hook in indicated st and draw up a loop, yo, and draw through 2 loops on hook; (2nd leg) yo, insert hook in next st and draw up a loop, yo and draw through 2 loops on hook, yo and draw through 3 remaining loops on hook.

**Cl (cluster):** Yo, insert hook in indicated st and draw up a loop, yo and draw through 2 loops on hook, yo, insert hook in *same* st and draw up a loop, [yo and draw through 2 loops on hook] twice (2 loops remain on hook).

**2Cltog (2 clusters together):** (first leg) Cl in indicated st (2 loops remain on hook); (2nd leg) Cl in next indicated st (3 loops remain on hook), yo and draw through all 3 loops on hook.

**3Cltog (3 clusters together):** (first leg) Cl in indicated st (2 loops remain on hook); (2nd leg) Cl in next indicated st (3 loops remain on hook); (3rd leg) Cl in next indicated st (4 loops remain on hook), yo and draw through all 4 loops on hook.

---

NOTE: Hat and flower are worked with right side facing at all times. Do not turn at the end of rounds.

# CLOCHE
## Hat

Ch 3; slip st in first ch to form a ring.

**Round 1 (Right side):** Ch 3 (counts as dc here and throughout), 10 dc in ring; join with a slip st in top of beginning ch-3 – 11 dc.

**Round 2:** Ch 3, dc in same st as join, 2 dc in each remaining dc around; join with a slip st in top of beginning ch-3 – 22 dc.

**Round 3:** Ch 2, Beg-Cl working first leg in same st as join, ch 3, Cl in back bar *(Fig. 3, page 44)* of 3rd ch from hook (*horizontal Cl made – 2 loops remain on hook*), Cl in same st as 2nd leg of previous Beg-Cl (3 loops remain on hook), Cl in next dc, yo and draw through all 4 loops on hook, *ch 3, 3Cltog working first leg in back bar of 3rd ch from hook, 2nd leg in same dc as last leg of previous Cl, and 3rd leg in next dc; repeat from * 18 more times, ch 3, 3Cltog working first leg in back bar of 3rd ch from hook, 2nd leg in same dc as last leg of previous Cl, and 3rd leg in slip st join of previous round, ch 3, Beg-Cl in back bar of 3rd ch from hook; join with a slip st in base of first horizontal Cl – 22 horizontal Cl.

**Rounds 4-12:** Ch 2, 2Cltog working first leg in same st as join and 2nd leg at base of next horizontal Cl, *ch 3, 3Cltog working first leg in back bar of 3rd ch from hook, 2nd leg in same st as last leg of previous Cl, and 3rd leg in base of next horizontal Cl; repeat from * 18 more times, ch 3, 3Cltog working first leg in back bar of 3rd ch from hook, 2nd leg in same st as last leg of previous Cl, and 3rd leg in slip st join of previous round, ch 3, Beg-Cl in back bar of 3rd ch from hook; join with a slip st in base of first horizontal Cl – 22 horizontal Cl. Fasten off.

## Flower

Ch 3; slip st in first ch to form a ring.

**Round 1 (Right side):** [Sc in ring, ch 3] 6 times; join with a slip st in first ch-3 space – 6 sc and 6 ch-3 spaces.

**Round 2:** Ch 1, 5 sc in each ch-3 space around; join with a slip st in first sc – 6 petals.

**Round 3:** Working behind the petals of Round 2, [slip st around post of next sc of Round 1 *(Fig. 2)*, ch 3] 6 times; join with a slip st in first ch-3 space.

**Fig. 2**

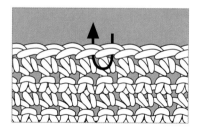

**Round 4:** Ch 1, (sc, hdc, 3 dc, hdc, sc) in each ch-3 space around; join with a slip st in first sc – 6 petals.

**Round 5:** Working behind petals of Round 4, ch 5, [skip next sc of Round 4, slip st around post of next sc of Round 4, ch 5] 5 times; join with a slip st in first ch-5 space.

**Round 6:** Ch 1, (sc, hdc, 5 dc, hdc, sc) in each ch-5 space around; join with a slip st in first sc – 6 petals. Fasten off.

## Finishing

Fold back brim. Using photograph as a guide, sew flower to hat. Weave in ends.

# Cozy Soft Baby Cocoon & Hat

Designed by Kim Kotary.

⬤◼☐☐ **EASY**

**Size:** Newborn to 3 months

**Finished Measurements**
Cocoon Circumference: 24" (61 cm)
Hat Circumference: 18" (45.5 cm)

## SHOPPING LIST

### Yarn (Bulky Weight)
RED HEART® Buttercup®
☐ 4277 Light Mint Multi - 4 balls

### Crochet Hook
☐ 6.5 mm [US K-10.5]

### Additional Supplies
☐ Split-lock stitch markers - 2
☐ Yarn needle

## GAUGE INFORMATION

9 sc and 8 rounds = 4" (10 cm).
**CHECK YOUR GAUGE. Use any size hook to obtain the gauge.**

## COCOON
### Bottom

**Round 1 (Right side):** Beginning at lower edge, ch 9, sc in 2nd ch from hook and in next 6 chs, 3 sc in last ch, place marker in center sc of the last 3 sc; working on opposite side of ch *(Fig. 6b, page 45)*, sc in next 6 chs, 2 sc in last ch, place marker in last sc made – 18 sc.

Do not join but work in continuous rounds. Move markers up each round.

**Next Round:** [Sc in each sc to 1 sc before marked sc, 2 sc in next sc, sc in marked sc] twice – 20 sc.

Repeat last round until there are 54 sc.

### Body

Work even on 54 sc until 21" (53.5 cm) from beginning.
Fasten off.
Weave in ends. Fold top edge down for cuff.

# HAT

## Crown

**Round 1 (Right side):** Beginning at top of hat, ch 5, sc in 2nd ch from hook and in next 2 chs, 3 sc in last ch, place marker in center sc of the last 3 sc; working on opposite side of ch *(Fig. 6b, page 45)*, sc in next 2 chs, 2 sc in last ch, place marker in last sc made − 10 sc.

Do not join but work in continuous rounds. Move markers up each round.

**Next Round:** [Sc in each sc to 1 sc before marked sc, 2 sc in next sc, sc in marked sc] twice − 12 sc.

Repeat last round until there are 42 sc.

## Body

Work even on 42 sc until 8" (20.5 cm) from beginning.
Fasten off.
Weave in ends. Fold bottom edge up for cuff.

# Beginner Mittens for All

Designed by Nancy Anderson.

 **EASY**

## SHOPPING LIST

### Yarn (Medium Weight) 4 MEDIUM

**RED HEART® Super Saver®**

**Child's Version:**
- ☐ 0387 Soft Navy **B** - 1 skein
- ☐ 0984 Shaded Dusk **C** - 1 skein

**Women's Version:**
- ☐ 0624 Tea Leaf **A** - 1 skein
- ☐ 0387 Soft Navy **B** - 1 skein

**Men's Version:**
- ☐ 0624 Tea Leaf **A** - 1 skein

### Crochet Hook
- ☐ 5.5 mm [US I-9]

### Additional Supplies
- ☐ Yarn needle

# SIZE INFORMATION

**Finished Measurements**

Child's Version:

6" (15 cm) around x
7½" (19 cm) long

Women's Version:

7½" (19 cm) around x
11½" (29 cm) long

Men's Version: 9½" (24 cm)
around x 12" (30.5 cm) long

*Size Note:* Directions are written
in Blue for size Small (child's
4/5 years), in Pink for size Medium
(women's), and in Green for size
Large (Men's). Directions written
in Black apply to all sizes.

# GAUGE INFORMATION

16 sc and 17 rows/rounds = 4"
(10 cm). **CHECK YOUR GAUGE.
Use any size hook to obtain the
gauge.**

——— **SPECIAL STITCH** ———

**sc2tog (single crochet
2 together):** [Insert hook in next
st, yo, draw yarn through st] twice,
yo, draw yarn through all 3 loops
on hook.

**NOTE:** These simple mittens are
designed without a definite left
or right hand and are worked in
joined rounds.

Cuffs are done in ribbed stitch
rows by working sc in the back
loops only. They are extra long for
added warmth or can be folded at
the wrist.

Men's mittens are worked in a
solid color, Child's and Women's in
stripe patterns as follows:
Work in 2 rounds of stripes for
Child's mittens *(Fig. 5a, page 44)*,
ending with 5 rounds of **C** at
fingertips.
Work in 1 round of stripes for
Women's mittens *(Fig. 5a,
page 44)*, ending with 7 rounds of
**A** at fingertips.

# MITTEN (Make 2)
## Cuff
Using C{B-A}, ch 15{21-24}.

**Row 1:** Working in back loops only *(Fig. 4, page 44)*, sc in 2nd ch from hook and each ch across; ch 1, turn.

Repeat Row 1 for a total of 18{22-24} rows.

Fold cuff in half and join ends with slip st to form cuff. Do not fasten off.

## Hand
**Round 1 (Right side):** Working along row ends on cuff, slip st evenly around for 18{22-26} sts; join with a slip st in first slip st.

**Round 2:** Ch 1, [sc in next 8{10-12} sts, 2 sc in next st] twice; join with a slip st in first sc – 20{24-28} sts.

**Round 3:** Ch 1, [sc in next 9{11-13} sts, 2 sc in next st] twice; join with a slip st in first sc – 22{26-30} sts.

**Round 4:** Ch 1, [sc in next 10{12-14} sts, 2 sc in next st] twice; join with a slip st in first sc – 24{28-32} sts.

**Women's Size ONLY**
**Round 5:** Ch 1, [sc in next 13 sts, 2 sc in next st] twice; join with a slip st in first sc – 30 sts.

**Men's Size ONLY**
**Round 5:** Ch 1, [sc in next 15 sts, 2 sc in next st] twice; join with a slip st in first sc – 34 sts.

**Round 6:** Ch 1, [sc in next 16 sts, 2 sc in next st] twice; join with a slip st in first sc – 36 sts.

**Round 7:** Ch 1, [sc in next 17 sts, 2 sc in next st] twice; join with a slip st in first sc – 38 sts.

**All Sizes:** Continuing with stripe/solid pattern as set, ch 1, sc in each st around; join with a slip st in first sc.
Repeat for a total of 1{3-3} round(s).

**THUMB OPENING**
**Next Round:** Ch 1, sc in next 20{26-32} sts, ch 4{5-6}; skip remaining sts and join with a slip st in first sc.

31

## UPPER HAND

Ch 1, sc in each st around for 8{10-12} rounds [24{31-38} sts], decreasing 1 st on last round for Women's size ONLY; join with a slip st in first sc – 24{30-38} sts.

**Round 1:** Ch 1, [sc in next 10{13-17} sts, sc2tog] twice; join with a slip st in first sc – 22{28-36} sts.

**Round 2:** Ch 1, [sc in next 9{12-16} sts, sc2tog] twice; join with a slip st in first sc – 20{26-34} sts.

**Round 3:** Ch 1, [sc in next 8{11-15} sts, sc2tog] twice; join with a slip st in first sc – 18{24-32} sts.

**Round 4:** Ch 1, [sc in next 7{10-14} sts, sc2tog] twice; join with a slip st in first sc – 16{22-30} sts.

### Child's Size ONLY
**Round 5:** Ch 1, sc2tog around; join with a slip st in first st – 8 sts. Fasten off. Continue with thumb.

### Women's & Men's Size ONLY
**Round 5:** Ch 1, sc in each st around; join with a slip st in first sc.

**Round 6:** Ch 1, [sc in next {9-13} sts, sc2tog] twice; join with a slip st in first sc – {20-28} sts.

**Rounds 7 and 8:** Ch 1, sc2tog around; join with a slip st in first st – {5-7} sts. Fasten off at end of Round 8.

### THUMB - All Sizes
**Round 1:** Join yarn to thumb opening at st closest to upper hand; ch 1, sc in each st around; join with a slip st in first sc – 8{9-12} sts.

Sc in each st around for 4{7-8} rounds.

**Next Round:** Ch 1, sc2tog, sc around to last 2 sts, sc2tog – 6{7-10} sts.

**Last Round:** Ch 1, sc2tog around, working last st as sc on Women's size – 3{4-5} sts. Fasten off.

Weave in ends.

# Colorful Texting Gloves

Designed by Sara Delaney.

 **INTERMEDIATE**

**Size:** One size fits most

## SHOPPING LIST

**Yarn** (Super Fine)
**RED HEART® Heart & Sole®**
☐ 3931 Berry Bliss - 2 balls

### Crochet Hook
☐ 3.25 mm [US D-4]

### Additional Supplies
☐ Stitch markers
☐ ¼" (6 mm) Buttons - 4
☐ Yarn needle

# GAUGE INFORMATION

18 sts and 16 rounds = 4" (10 cm) in pattern. **CHECK YOUR GAUGE. Use any size hook to obtain the gauge.**

NOTE: Index fingers and thumbs flip back and are buttoned open while using phone.

## ──SPECIAL STITCHES──

**Fsc (foundation single crochet):** (first st) Ch 2, insert hook under top 2 strands of first ch, yo, draw up a loop, yo, draw through 1 loop, yo, draw through both loops **(first fsc complete)**. (remaining sts) Insert hook under both loops of previous st, yo, draw up a loop, yo, draw through 1 loop, yo, draw through both loops.

**esc (extended single crochet):** Insert hook into the next st, yo and draw up a loop, yo and draw through 1 loop, yo and draw through both loops.

**esc2tog (extended single crochet 2 together):** Insert hook under front loop only of next 2 sts *(Fig. 4, page 44)*, yo and draw a loop through both sts, yo and draw through 1 loop, yo and draw through both loops.

**FPsc (front post single crochet):** Yo and insert hook from front to back and to front again around the vertical post of indicated st *(Fig. 7, page 45)*, yo and draw up a loop. (There are now 3 loops on your hook.) Yo and draw through 2 loops on your hook. (There will be 2 loops left on the hook.) Yo and draw through the last 2 loops on your hook.

**BPsc (back post single crochet):** Yo and insert hook from back to front and to back again around the vertical post of indicated st *(Fig. 7, page 45)*, yo and draw up a loop. (There are now 3 loops on your hook.) Yo and draw through 2 loops on your hook. (There will be 2 loops left on the hook.) Yo and draw through the last 2 loops on your hook.

# GLOVE (Make 2)
## Hand

**Foundation Round:** Fsc 30; join in a round with a slip st.

**Round 1 (Right side):** Ch 2, esc in each st around; join with a slip st to the 2nd ch of beginning ch-2.

**Round 2:** Ch 2, FPsc in first st, BPsc in 2nd st, *FPsc in next st, BPsc in next st; repeat from * around; join with a slip st to the 2nd ch of beginning ch-2.

**Rounds 3 and 4:** Repeat Round 2 twice.

**Round 5:** Ch 2, esc in each st around; join with a slip st to the 2nd ch of beginning ch-2 – 30 sts.

**Round 6:** Ch 2, 2 esc in next st, esc in each st around to last 2 sts, 2 esc in next st, esc in last st; join with a slip st to the 2nd ch of beginning ch-2 – 32 sts.

**Rounds 7 and 8:** Repeat Rounds 5 and 6 – 34 sts.

**Rounds 9 and 10:** Repeat Rounds 5 and 6 – 36 sts.

**Rounds 11 and 12:** Repeat Rounds 5 and 6 – 38 sts.

**Rounds 13 and 14:** Repeat Rounds 5 and 6 – 40 sts.

**Rounds 15 and16:** Repeat Rounds 5 and 6 – 42 sts.

**Rounds 17 and 18:** Ch 2, esc in each st around; join with a slip st to the 2nd ch of beginning ch-2.

**Round 19:** Ch 2, esc in next 38 sts, esc into the post of the last esc made, place a marker in this st (counts as a ch-2) round complete.

**Round 20:** Skip the last 4 sts of the last round, esc into the 5th st of the round just finished (you just set aside sts for the thumb that will be worked later), esc in the next 33 sts; join the round with a slip st to the esc with the marker – 34 sts.

**Round 21:** Ch 2, esc in each st around; join with a slip st to the 2nd ch of beginning ch 2 – 34 sts.

**Rounds 22, 24, and 26:** Repeat Round 21.

**Round 23:** Ch 2, 2 esc in next st, esc in each st around to last 2 sts, 2 esc in next st, esc in last st; join with a slip st to the 2nd ch of beginning ch-2 – 36 sts.

**Round 25:** Ch 2, 2 esc in next st, esc in each st around to last 2 sts, 2 esc in next st, esc in last st; join with a slip st to the 2nd ch of beginning ch-2 – 38 sts.

**Round 27:** Ch 2, esc in next 15 sts, skip next 8 sts, esc in last 15 sts; join with a slip st to the 2nd ch of beginning ch-2 (you just set aside the sts for the pinkie that will be worked later) – 30 sts.

**Round 28:** Ch 2, esc in next 10 sts, skip next 10 sts, esc in last 10 sts; join with a slip st to the 2nd ch of beginning ch-2 (you just set aside the sts for the ring finger that will be worked later) – 20 sts.

**Round 29:** Ch 2, esc in next 5 sts, [esc into the post of the last st] twice, skip next 10 sts, esc in last 5 sts; join with a slip st to the 2nd ch of beginning ch-2 (you just set aside the sts for the middle finger that will be worked later) – 12 sts.

## INDEX FINGER
**Round 30:** Ch 2, esc in each st around; join with a slip st to the 2nd ch of beginning ch-2 – 12 sts.

**Rounds 31-37:** Repeat Round 30.

### For The Right Hand
**Round 38:** Ch 2, esc in next 6 sts, esc through the back loop only *(Fig. 4, page 44)* of next 6 sts (across back of hand); join with a slip st to the 2nd ch of beginning ch-2 – 12 sts.

### For The Left Hand
**Round 38:** Ch 2, esc through the back loop only *(Fig. 4, page 44)* of next 6 sts (across back of hand), esc in next 6 sts; join with a slip st to the 2nd ch of beginning ch-2 – 12 sts.

### For Both Hands
**Round 39:** Ch 2, esc in each st around; join with a slip st to the 2nd ch of beginning ch-2. Fasten off. Weave in ends.

## FINGERTIP

**Round 1:** Join yarn to remaining front loop *(Fig. 6a, page 45)* of the first esc that was worked through the back loop only in Round 38; ch 2 and esc through the same front loop, esc through the front loop only of the next 5 sts, [work esc in the post of the last st] 6 times, being careful not to twist; join with slip st to the 2nd ch of beginning ch-2 – 12 sts.

**Rounds 2-4:** Ch 2, esc in each st around; join with a slip st to the 2nd ch of beginning ch-2 – 12 sts.

**Round 5:** Ch 2, [esc2tog] 6 times; join with a slip st to the 2nd ch of beginning ch-2, ch 4, slip st in joined st (this creates button loop). Fasten off, weave tail through the top of all sts and tighten to close. Weave in ends.

## MIDDLE FINGER

**Round 1:** Join yarn between 2 sts at the base of the index finger facing the middle finger; ch 2, esc in the 5th st of Round 28 (same as the base of the index finger), esc in next 10 sts, esc in the 15th st of Round 28 (again, same as the base of the index finger); join with a slip st to the 2nd ch of beginning ch-2 – 12 sts.

**Rounds 2-13:** Ch 2, esc in each st around; join with a slip st to the 2nd ch of beginning ch-2 – 12 sts.

**Round 14:** Ch 2, [esc2tog] 6 times; join with a slip st to the 2nd ch of beginning ch-2. Fasten off, weave tail through the top of all sts and tighten to close. Weave in ends.

## RING FINGER

**Round 1:** Join yarn through the posts of both sts at the base of the middle finger, facing the ring finger; ch 2, esc in the 10th st of Round 27 (same as the base of the middle finger), esc in next 10 sts, esc in the 21st st of Round 27 (again, same as the base of the middle finger); join with a slip st to the 2nd ch of beginning ch-2 – 12 sts.

**Rounds 2-12:** Ch 2, esc in each st around; join with a slip st to the 2nd ch of beginning ch-2 – 12 sts.

**Round 13:** Ch 2, [esc2tog] 6 times; join with a slip st to the 2nd ch of beginning ch-2. Fasten off, weave tail through the top of all sts and tighten to close. Weave in ends.

## PINKIE

**Round 1:** Join yarn through the posts of both sts at the base of the ring finger, facing the pinkie finger; ch 2, esc in the 15th st of Round 26 (same as the base of the ring finger), esc in next 8 sts, esc in the 24th st of Round 26 (again, same as the base of the ring finger); join with a slip st to the 2nd ch of beginning ch-2 – 10 sts.

**Rounds 2-8:** Ch 2, esc in each st around; join with a slip st to the 2nd ch of beginning ch-2 – 10 sts.

**Round 9:** Ch 2, [esc2tog] 5 times; join with a slip st to the 2nd ch of beginning ch-2. Fasten off, weave tail through the top of all sts and tighten to close. Weave in ends.

There may be small gaps at the base of the fingers; use yarn tails to weave closed.

## THUMB

**Round 1:** This round of the thumb was begun in Round 20 of the hand (ch 2 and 4 esc already exist). Join yarn to the 5th st of Round 20, ch 2 (this counts as an esc), 2 esc in the 38th st of Round 19, esc in the next 3 sts, 2 esc in last st; join with a slip st to the 2nd ch of beginning ch-2 – 12 sts.

**Rounds 2-6:** Ch 2, esc in each st around; join with a slip st to the 2nd ch of beginning ch-2 – 12 sts.

### For The Right Hand

**Round 7:** Ch 2, esc in next 6 sts, esc through the back loop only of next 6 sts; join with a slip st to the 2nd ch of beginning ch-2 – 12 sts.

**For The Left Hand**
**Round 7:** Ch 2, esc through the back loop only of next 6 sts, esc in next 6 sts; join with a slip st to the 2nd ch of beginning ch-2 – 12 sts.

**For Both Hands**
**Round 8:** Ch 2, esc in each st around; join with a slip st to the 2nd ch of beginning ch-2. Fasten off and weave in ends.

**THUMB TIP**
**Round 1:** Join yarn to the remaining front loop of the first esc that was worked through the back loop only in Round 7; ch 2 and esc through the same front loop, esc through the front loop only of the next 5 sts, [work esc in the post of the last st] 6 times; being careful not to twist, join with a slip st to the 2nd ch of beginning ch-2 – 12 sts.

**Rounds 2-4:** Ch 2, esc in each st around; join with a slip st to the 2nd ch of beginning ch-2 – 12 sts.

**Round 5:** Ch 2, [esc2tog] 6 times; join with a slip st to the 2nd ch of beginning ch-2, ch 4, slip st in joined st (buttonhole made). Fasten off, weave tail through the top of all sts and tighten to close. Weave in ends.

## Finishing
Lay the index finger and thumb tips back against hand and mark the st that lies underneath the buttonhole loop at the tip; sew buttons at these points.

# General Instructions

## ABBREVIATIONS

| | |
|---|---|
| Beg-Cl | Beginning Cluster |
| BPsc | Back Post single crochet(s) |
| 2Cltog | 2 Clusters together |
| 3Cltog | 3 Clusters together |
| ch(s) | chain(s) |
| Cl | Cluster(s) |
| cm | centimeters |
| dc | double crochet(s) |
| dc2tog | double crochet 2 together |
| esc | extended single crochet(s) |
| esc2tog | extended single crochet 2 together |
| FPsc | Front Post single crochet(s) |
| Fsc | Foundation single crochet(s) |
| hdc | half double crochet(s) |
| mm | millimeters |
| sc | single crochet(s) |
| sc2tog | single crochet 2 together |
| st(s) | stitch(es) |
| yo | yarn over |

| CROCHET HOOKS | | | | | | | | | | | | | | | |
|---|---|---|---|---|---|---|---|---|---|---|---|---|---|---|---|
| U.S. | B-1 | C-2 | D-3 | E-4 | F-5 | G-6 | H-8 | I-9 | J-10 | K-10½ | L-11 | M/N-13 | N/P-15 | P/Q | Q | S |
| Metric - mm | 2.25 | 2.75 | 3.25 | 3.5 | 3.75 | 4 | 5 | 5.5 | 6 | 6.5 | 8 | 9 | 10 | 15 | 16 | 19 |

# SYMBOLS & TERMS

\* or \*\* — repeat whatever follows the \* or \*\* as indicated.

( ) or [ ] — work directions given in parentheses or brackets the number of times specified.

work even — work without increasing or decreasing in the established pattern.

| CROCHET TERMINOLOGY | | |
|---|---|---|
| UNITED STATES | | INTERNATIONAL |
| slip stitch (slip st) | = | single crochet (sc) |
| single crochet (sc) | = | double crochet (dc) |
| half double crochet (hdc) | = | half treble crochet (htr) |
| double crochet (dc) | = | treble crochet(tr) |
| treble crochet (tr) | = | double treble crochet (dtr) |
| double treble crochet (dtr) | = | triple treble crochet (ttr) |
| triple treble crochet (tr tr) | = | quadruple treble crochet (qtr) |
| skip | = | miss |

| Yarn Weight Symbol & Names | LACE 0 | SUPER FINE 1 | FINE 2 | LIGHT 3 | MEDIUM 4 | BULKY 5 | SUPER BULKY 6 |
|---|---|---|---|---|---|---|---|
| Type of Yarns in Category | Fingering, 10-count crochet thread | Sock, Fingering Baby | Sport, Baby | DK, Light Worsted | Worsted, Afghan, Aran | Chunky, Craft, Rug | Bulky, Roving |
| Crochet Gauge* Ranges in Single Crochet to 4" (10 cm) | 32-42 double crochets** | 21-32 sts | 16-20 sts | 12-17 sts | 11-14 sts | 8-11 sts | 5-9 sts |
| Advised Hook Size Range | Steel*** 6,7,8 Regular hook B-1 | B-1 to E-4 | E-4 to 7 | 7 to I-9 | I-9 to K-10.5 | K-10.5 to M-13 | M-13 and larger |

*GUIDELINES ONLY: The chart above reflects the most commonly used gauges and hook sizes for specific yarn categories.

** Lace weight yarns are usually crocheted on larger-size hooks to create lacy openwork patterns. Accordingly, a gauge range is difficult to determine. Always follow the gauge stated in your pattern.

*** Steel crochet hooks are sized differently from regular hooks–the higher the number the smaller the hook, which is the reverse of regular hook sizing.

| | |
|---|---|
| ■□□□ BEGINNER | Projects for first-time crocheters using basic stitches. Minimal shaping. |
| ■■□□ EASY | Projects using yarn with basic stitches, repetitive stitch patterns, simple color changes, and simple shaping and finishing. |
| ■■■□ INTERMEDIATE | Projects using a variety of techniques, such as basic lace patterns or color patterns, mid-level shaping and finishing. |
| ■■■■ EXPERIENCED | Projects with intricate stitch patterns, techniques and dimension, such as non-repeating patterns, multi-color techniques, fine threads, small hooks, detailed shaping and refined finishing. |

## GAUGE

Gauge refers to the number of stitches and rows or rounds in a given area. When making projects, ensure that your project is the correct finished size and is to gauge. Working the area as stated in the pattern and then measure to check that it agrees with the gauge given. If it is not the same size, change your hook size. If the area is too large, use a smaller hook. If the area is too small, use a larger hook size.

## BACK BAR

Work only in loops indicated by arrows *(Fig. 3)*.

**Fig. 3**

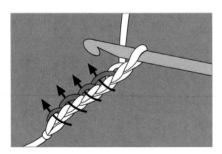

## BACK OR FRONT LOOP ONLY

Work only in loop(s) indicated by arrow *(Fig. 4)*.

**Fig. 4**

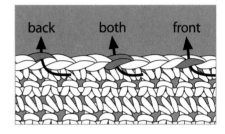

## CHANGING COLORS

Work the last stitch to within one step of completion, hook new yarn *(Fig. 5a or 5b)* and draw through all loops on the hook.

**Fig. 5a**

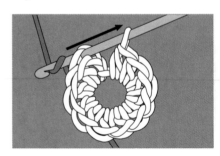

**Fig. 5b**

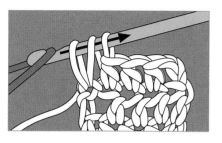

When instructed to work in free loops of a chain or opposite side of a chain, work in loop indicated by arrow *(Fig. 6b)*.

**Fig. 6b**

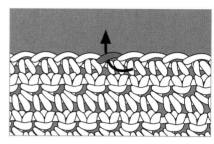

## FREE LOOPS

After working in back or front loops only on a row or round, there will be a ridge of unused loops. These are called the free loops or the remaining loops. Later, when instructed to work in the free loops or remaining loops of the same row or round, work in these loops *(Fig. 6a)*.

## POST STITCH

Work around post of stitch indicated, inserting hook in direction of arrow *(Fig. 7)*.

**Fig. 6a**

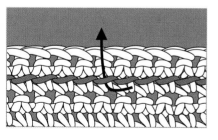

**Fig. 7**

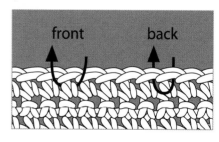

front        back

# POMPOM

Cut a piece of cardboard 3" (7.5 cm) wide and as long as you want
the diameter of your finished pompom to be.

Wind the yarn around the cardboard until it is approximately ½" (12 mm)
thick in the middle *(Fig. 8a)*. Carefully slip the yarn off the cardboard and
firmly tie an 18" (45.5 cm) length of yarn around the middle *(Fig. 8b)*.
Leave yarn ends long enough to attach the pompom. Cut the loops on
both ends and trim the pompom into a smooth ball *(Fig. 8c)*.

**Fig. 8a**

**Fig. 8b**

**Fig. 8c**

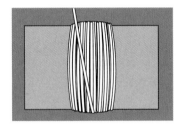
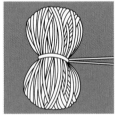
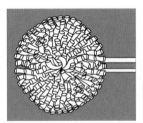

# Yarn Information

The projects in this book were created with **RED HEART®** yarns. For best results, we recommend following the pattern exactly as written. Be sure to purchase the amounts recommended in the pattern, and retain your labels. Always follow the care instructions provided on the label.

 **MEDIUM WEIGHT YARN**
**RED HEART® Soft®**, Art. E728
available in solid colors 5 oz (141 g), 256 yd (234 m); in prints 4 oz (113 g), 204 yd (187 m); and in heathers 4 oz (113 g), 212 yd (194 m) balls.

 **MEDIUM WEIGHT YARN**
**RED HEART® With Love®**, Art. E400 available in solid colors 7 oz (198 g), 370 yd (338 m); and in multis 5 oz (141 g), 230 yd (211 m) skeins.

 **MEDIUM WEIGHT YARN**
**RED HEART® Super Saver® Econo**, Art. E300 available in solid colors 7 oz (198 g), 364 yd (333 m); in prints, multis & heathers 5 oz (141 g), 244 yd (223 m); and in flecks 5 oz (141 g), 260 yd (238 m) skeins.

**BULKY WEIGHT YARN**
**RED HEART® Buttercup®,**
Art. N396 available in 1.76 oz
(50 g), 63 yd (57 m) balls.

**SUPER FINE WEIGHT YARN**
**RED HEART® Heart & Sole®,**
Art. E745 available in multi colors
1.76 oz (50 g), 213 yd (195 m) balls.

## For more ideas & inspiration –

www.redheart.com ▪ www.facebook.com/redheartyarns
www.pinterest.com/redheartyarns ▪ www.twitter.com/redheartyarns
www.youtube.com/redheartyarns ▪ Instagram @redheartyarns